THE PASSION OF LIZZIE BORDEN:

NEW AND SELECTED POEMS

Also by Ruth Whitman

BLOOD & MILK POEMS

AN ANTHOLOGY OF MODERN YIDDISH POETRY
(bilingual, translated and selected)

THE MARRIAGE WIG AND OTHER POEMS

THE SELECTED POEMS OF JACOB GLATSTEIN
(translated, with introduction)

The Passion of Lizzie Borden: New and Selected Poems

BY RUTH WHITMAN

October House Inc

Some of these poems first appeared in *The Antioch Review, Arion's Dolphin, The Atlantic Monthly, Boston Review of the Arts, The Carleton Miscellany, The Chicago Tribune, Commentary,* the Editor, *The Harvard Advocate, Hellcoal Anthology One, The Impressions Workshop, The Kenyon Review, The Literary Review, The Massachusetts Review, Midstream, The Nation, The New Republic, The New York Quarterly, The New York Times, Poetry Northwest, The Prairie Schooner, The Tuftonian, The United Church Herald, Yankee.* "Dead Center" appeared originally in *The New Yorker;* "The Lost Steps" and "A Spider on My Poem" in *Poetry.*

Poems from THE MARRIAGE WIG are reprinted by permission of Harcourt Brace Jovanovich, Inc., © 1964, 1965, 1966, 1967, 1968, by Ruth Whitman.

October House Inc.
160 Sixth Avenue
New York, N.Y. 10013
Printed in the United States of America
Library of Congress Catalog Number 78-150240
SBN Cloth 8079-0183-0; Paper 8079-0184-9

Contents

THE PASSION OF LIZZIE BORDEN

The Passion of Lizzie Borden 11
Translating 20
Bread Loaf 1941
    1. R. F. 22
    2. On Theodore Roethke's Lap 23
    3. Rebuilding the House 24
In the Vatican Museum 1952 25
Among the Green Mansions 1936 27
Playing Dead 28
For David Sacks, Odessa 1881–Boston 1965 29
Utterance 30
A Nap at Sunion 31
Digging 32
Zion 34
The Third Wedding 35
Four Poems of Comfort and Discomfort
    1. After the Abortion 36
    2. On the Way to Mount Auburn Hospital 37
    3. Derailed 38
    4. Bellyache 39
Rising to the Occasion 40
When the Child at Your Breast Is a Metaphor 41
A Cry 42
K. 516 43
Painter 44
Laying a Fire 45
Meditation 46
Lament for a Yiddish Poet 47
Castoff Skin 51
Passover 1970 52

from THE MARRIAGE WIG (1968)

A Spider on My Poem 57
Tall Grasses 58
Spring 59
Listening to grownups quarreling 60
Persephone Travels Back to Hell, as Arranged 61
Rachel Waking 63
Cutting the Jewish Bride's Hair 64
The Marriage Wig 65
Ripeness 67
Reunion 68
David's Breath 69
Summer Thunderstorms 70
Sitting for a Picture 71
The Act of Bread 72
She Doesn't Want to Bring the
    Tides in Any More 74
All My Bicycles Are Emily Dickinson 75
Sister Pharaoh 76
The Nun Cuts Her Hair 77
Dancing at Delphi 78
Noonday in the Plaka 79
Public Images 80
Her Delirium 83
The Mark 84
Dead Center 85
In the Smoking Car 86
Old Houses 87
I Become My Grandfather 88
Departures 89
You Outlive All Your Diseases Except One 91
Shoring Up 93

from BLOOD & MILK POEMS (1963)

Stealing Forsythia 97
Elevator 98
Round 99
Nuns on the Beach 100
The Witch of the Wave 101
Song for a Vigil 103
The Old Man's Mistress 104
The Peacock Screams 106
Aubade 107
The Lost Steps 108
Her Life Was in My Hands 110
The Flowering Skull 111
Antiphonal 112
The Sea Flower 113
The Phoenix 114
My Daughter the Cypress 115
Touro Synagogue 116

THE PASSION OF LIZZIE BORDEN

The Passion of Lizzie Borden

On the morning of August 4, 1892, during an intense heat wave, Lizzie Borden's father and stepmother were found brutally murdered in their house in Fall River, Massachusetts. Their daughter Lizzie, a thirty-three-year-old spinster, secretary of the Young People's Society for Christian Endeavor and active in the Fruit and Flower Mission, was arrested for the murder, tried, and acquitted.

It is innate in the female psyche to bring blood, conception, birth and death into close connection with one another. . . .
—Helene Deutsch, *The Psychology of Women*

Q. I ask you again to explain to me why you took those pears from the pear tree. A. I did not take them from the pear tree. Q. From the ground. Wherever you took them from. I thank you for correcting me; going into the barn, going upstairs into the hottest place in the barn, in the rear of the barn, the hottest place, and there standing and eating those pears that morning?
—Inquest testimony of Miss Lizzie Borden,
Fall River, August 9-11, 1892

We were talking in the afternoon, me and Lizzie Borden, and I says, "I can tell you one thing you can't do," and she says, "Tell me what it is, Mrs. Reagan." I says, "Break an egg, Miss Borden," and she says, "Break an egg?" I says, "Yes." "Well," she says, "I can break an egg." I says, "Not the way I would tell you to break it. . . ." And she did get the egg, and she got it in her hands, and she couldn't break it, and she says, "There," she says, "that is the first thing that I undertook to do that I never could."
—Testimony of Mrs. Hannah Reagan, matron
at the Fall River police station, on the
ninth day of the trial, New Bedford,
June 14, 1893

The Passion of Lizzie Borden

1.

Heat cracks the skin of Fall River.
Soot hangs flat
over the moist city.

Pears
sweat in the backyard.
Sitting alone in the kitchen

Lizzie feels
chunks of leftover mutton
heavy in her

belly. Her father
has left for the bank. The ring
he gave her long ago

pinches her finger.

2.

Openeyed last night she felt
her blood pounding
the back of her neck,

       tidal waves from the sea
       that poured up the Taunton river,
       tore open the breakwater,
       ripped apart her corsets
       and pumped breath, air,
       sealife into her,

sunstorms, volcanoes, astral debris,
until she was pregnant with a pregnancy
that puts an end to wishing.

3.

She woke, thicker around the shoulders, heavier
under the jaw. The birds
had left the burning pear tree.

This house has killed the girl she was.
Narrow, gray, grudging in windows,
bare of guests or laughing,

the parlor's only pleasure is to lay out
corpses or tell tales of each new
disease, step by fatal step.

What holds her here, eating pears?

4.

In the August heat
she irons handkerchiefs for her stepmother,
heating the iron on the kitchen fire
in the black stove.

The center of the earth is always boiling,
and she must have the trick of eye to see
how she can liquefy
stones, trees,
slash air so she can breathe,
take life to make life, break
the blind wall open with her fist.

5.

She'll hurl this pear against the door
until its ripe meat splatters,
like flesh torn in handfuls from the bone.

She'll trap rage in her like a cage
trapping a bear. Not only where
her sex is, but where her veins
become its bars.

She'll think, as it draws her juice
to her nipples: *that channel is why*
I was made.
My roots curl under me
where they suck life
(I'll find the sun
I'll husband a flowering bough)

6.

this sprung and spiralled wrath
won't uncoil till she's invented death

Her father is napping in the parlor,
her stepmother is sitting
at the vanity upstairs.

7.

Shake the murderous mountains and dance
a step or two before you turn to rain.

Then in the sky that gives you lightning,
in that same sky
your meteor will hurl;
will singe the tops of trees and bring
spring to the dry hedges of the moon
and set a clanging in the world
and break
by twos
the timbrels of the stars.

> *Who's to judge me? When I sleep I sleep
> curled on the shoulder of God*

8.

At last
I feel hallelujah in my hips
my son the day comes out of me the morning

She raises the ax.

Translating

for Jacob Glatstein

The old man was cold.
King David, they said,
we've heaped piles of clothes
on your bed, but your feet
are still icy, night after
night. Let us find you
a girl, a young
Shulamite, intelligent,
kind, who can spread
her warm bones
over you. . . .

                Abishag's
black hair lay
like a shawl on his throat,
her breasts and belly
and her rosy thighs
rode his flesh
shyly all night.

He did not enter her.

But as they lay,
slowly warming,
his voice found her ear,
and since he was sleepless,
he told her what
he was thinking:

how a slingshot had won him
a great lopsided battle
when he was a boy;

how he slew his ten thousands;
how his soul was knit
to his lover Jonathan;
how he answered Saul's
hatred with mercy;
how he danced unashamed
before the Ark
with songs and lyres
with harps and cymbals
and made his wife angry;
lusted after
married Bathsheba;
got himself children,
was betrayed
by a son, a son;
how songs still came
to him. . . .

      And Abishag,
after all those hours
of listening, the world
in his voice,
rose in the morning
full of spermatic words.

Bread Loaf 1941

1. R. F.

We drank beer, cheered
Schwartzkopf, rolled
in the mown meadow
and wondered
which poet to marry.

We played
on our plateau, heedless
of Hitler. And the
granddaddy
of us all,

shaggy as a bear,
wagged his white head.
His despair
was so wittily said,
we didn't care.

2. On Theodore Roethke's Lap

There was only one motion,
down, racing down the mountain
in a beatup Chevrolet

crammed with a zoo of poets
and fat round Ted,
the lowflying slug.

We clutched each other
inside that black box
feeling our way by guess

and by gosh, whizzing down past
devilmaycare trees and a brook
at the bottom of the gulch

calling its cool persuasion,
early death for nine young
geniuses, thirsty for beer.

Ted's large knees under
me, the smallest and youngest,
felt soft and warm.

"Remember?" I asked,
years later, "after your
papa's waltz?"

"I always got a hardon," he answered,
now almost at the bottom of the mountain,
the waters loud in his ears.

3. Rebuilding the House

On the flat lawn of silence
we will take each red brick,
   each yellow clapboard,
     and put back nail by nail
  like a film clip in reverse
a demolished Queen Anne house.

     The Olympic highjumper floats
   in the air like dandelion fluff
backward to his starting point.
And we will take each syllable,
   each movement of the mouth, tongue, jaw

    no, before that,
    the breath from the chest cavity,
   the smallest muscles to expel air, sound
waves, voice, word
and build the house that held the
first marriage room the poem.

In the Vatican Museum 1952

Through a glass box, behind an Attic vase,
love face, habitually misplaced,
how you turned up like a clown
in the museum in Rome,
looking through to us
at the same vase
in the same case in the same room,
far from Cambridge, Salt
Lake City, all your warring
and contrary places.

Awkward body born from a candy machine,
you appeared and disappeared, sad
smile on a mummer's face.

Young and naked in March
we all plunged together
into the cold Rockport quarries—
and you disappeared.
                              I found you

gaping over a halfeaten banana
at the Spreading Chestnut Tree on Brattle Street.
We captured you in our furnished room
over a bottle of chianti.

You disappeared.
                    Love,
in and out of windows, we

took a bus to Salem
and lost you again
among the seven gables.

                        Antic face
in the Vatican, how
did you come to be jumbled among
these antiquities?

Among the Green Mansions 1936

At the tea our mothers arranged
we two sat bored, you
in your fourteen-year-old
braids, me in my
prim chignon,
until we discovered
we both really lived below the neck
among the Green Mansions.

Afternoons by the river we waited
(you sitting on the wall,
an ocean liner waiting to be launched,
I a toy boat with nervous sails)—
scribbling poems of longing
and sudden rape—
like W. H. Hudson's jungle bird
glinting her breast
among the torrid trees.

Playing Dead

Locked in a motel
of mummy light,
fake air, we breathe
plastic.

       Thin dreams
flick across the walls.
Voices quarreling from the next tomb
keep us
not quite asleep.

A splinter of morning
enters through a crack.
We pry at the slit
until an untamed
tiger of sun springs in,
pushing the door open.

We have the answer
before the question.

For David Sacks, Odessa 1881—Boston 1965

Once in his jaunty middle age
his wife had caught him again behind the door
kissing the girl from downstairs. . . .

> Driving to the hospital we lied,
> They're going to make you well, you'll
> dance at our wedding.
>   His arm
> was still smooth as a boy's. You could hide
> your fingers in his thick
> eighty-four-year-old hair. Natty
> even in his hospital johnny,
> he basked in a flurry of nurses.
> But he no longer wanted to eat.

. . . Fighting years of cooking smoke,
counting children, pennies, sugarbabies
from the candy store she kept for him,
she locked him
                debonair as Odessa
in his room.

Utterance

Miss Muffet,
perceiving the spider
beside her,

screamed.
She moved the tiny muscles
in her adam's apple, dropped

her lower jaw, and forced the air
in waves
out of her mouth

to my eardrums,
a minute thrumming.
She knew, as her animal ancestors

before her, that sound
carries well, will turn a corner,
can be heard in the dark.

I think I hear
through a musky orchard
the silent abdominal

language of bees
playing violins
to the bass sonatas of whales

circling the sea.
I'm threading these songs
on syllables of wonder, remembering

bekos, the Phrygian word for bread.

A Nap at Sunion

Peeling away the layers of clouds,
dollying in with my dream camera,
I see

a girl
curled up naked
sleeping on a rock.

She has climbed down the spiney hill
to explore an ancient cave
chill with the smell of shepherd's urine and Poseidon.

She swims in the sea near a ledge,
never thinking of the octopus watching her.
She floats

toward adolescent islands
nippling the horizon.
And then she sleeps

while the horns
of the god's temple
rise over her.

Digging

centuries from now in the soil
of his city, the antiquarian will change
his story, partly guessing how rain
wore down the mountain
and how earth heaved up its double.

Layer on layer, the land doubles
back on itself. But all his digging
will not reveal the mountain
worn away or the soil
multiplied, or how rain
marries out his features. Change

comes atom by atom, an exchange
of smooth for rough, double
for unique. Each drop of rain
pocks the world's surface, digging
minuscule trenches in the soil
of mountains.

And the mountain
changes,
moving through air, water, soil,
like a juggler with a double
set of oranges. Digging
reveals he is not wholly lost, becoming rain.

The rain
pours down the mountain,
wearing away the scholar digging
through each change
of lifetime, through each double

city under soil,

wearing away the soil
itself. Pebbles rain
down, doubling
the ground he walks on. Mountains
of change
open beneath his digging.

Digging in the soil
of his city, he exchanges himself for his double:
atom, mountain, rain.

Zion

Grayfaced,
groping through the day,
I come to touch you breast to breast
and spring up, replenished, rosy
with your quickening.

Touchstone,
your body is my Israel,
your shoulder my wailing
wall, your face the bible
of my wandering.

The Third Wedding

On the way to her second wedding
dressed like a Christmas package
tinseled and laced with ribbon,
she caught a look at herself.

Her heart crashed with terror
under her champagne dress.
She shook from her shoes to her careful
veil.

      Where was the minyan
of ten good men? The cup
under the bridegroom's heel?
The canopy of flowers?

When guests turned to the altar,
she shed her mistaken skin
and rose clear of the building.
No one noticed her missing.

She gathered ten years for a minyan,
plucked a canopy of planets,
brought her body like a cup

to the bridegroom long denied
who drew her to his side,
his rib, his final bride.

Four Poems of Comfort and Discomfort

1. After the Abortion

Your knees, Uncle Doctor had said,
Watch those knees.

                    Traffic,
tuned to Schönberg,
floated through
the August window.

I tasted flat peroxide
and death.

On a certain betrayed afternoon
I realized
the bubbling was my own blood.
Half a lifetime later,

twenty miles away,
I leaned my head on my hand
and aged.

2. On the Way to Mount Auburn Hospital

Inside pain's white
balloon I tasted
every pebble and pothole
the narrow red truck
jerked over

The fireman beside me
with the vague family face
was saying something blurry,
but his hand holding mine
was dry and clear

3. Derailed

that time the train
    heeled and yawed
I braced my angry back

against foot-
    loose evil, my long expected
adversary

His dark flank
    passed over
me

Stumbling to the broken
    door
I discovered

    I had lost my shoe

4. Bellyache

The night she had a bellyache
    she fitted herself into
        all his corners

    and spaces, wearing
    him like a bandage
against her little pains.

    Curling behind him
    holding his sleeping penis
in her hand

        she tried to become
        part of his
        architecture.

Rising to the Occasion

Up! As Archilochus said,
soul, you must, despite all
annoyances, and this
vile island you live on, shaped
like the backbone of an ass:
despite this, up, wash, dress
and out.

Soul lies wallowing with a cold in his nose.
His head aches. Fever. Loving enemies
come running with pills, chicken, exotic
remedies. All night there's a chill in the room.
Fever. War.

Up! Beneath the island,
vomited up from ancient
volcanoes, there hides a grievous
fault. But splayfooted soul
will rise. His juice will spurt
again, again through a
dry stalk.

When the Child at Your Breast Is a Metaphor

1.

At the pool
the young mother in the yellow hat
follows along the edge,
on land,
watching her tadpole child in the water.
Every muscle in the mother's dry body
swims, as her child paddles across the surface,
not drowning. She can't keep her hands
from stretching out. She moves
her feet along the edge,
dancing a pas de deux of terror
and separateness.

2.

The child's voice on the telephone
wavers and breaks
as the rainstorm breaks on the line.
Thunder slams the house.
His words,
jigsawed by lightning,
fall
apart
while rain
beats in the open windows
blurring the words
in her ear.

A Cry

A man is howling like a dog.
Is a dog crying like a man?

In your backyard universe
where clusters of birds sang like roses and
crows rowing through the thick air
have dropped their triangular cries,
someone is in pain.

A dog thinks he is a man.
Or a man is skinned to his animal.

K. 516

From your graveyard
on the moon, three
hundred thousand
miles away, you
look back
on your leafy toy
(diminutive, savage
as a child, round
with baby fat
and dimples)
and you think of a pulse
in the throat of Constanze
in 1782,
a mote in the mote
in the eye of death,
and out of your cinders,
across your rubble of birthdays,
you jig her a rondo
allegro, the broken
wing of a fly.

Painter

What's riches to him
that has made a great peacock
with the pride of his eye?
                              YEATS

He sees into yellow balloons
          of sun.
                    Dives
into turquoise. Swims
          under layers of blue.

Turns and walks
          around the trunk of a tree
flat on the wall. Drops a cat

between   the sleeve
          and the rib
of the portrait.

          Sees space.

Six oceandeep miles of it
          in a narrow room.

Sees.

          And holds Cezanne's apple,
like love,
                    the round of it.

Laying a Fire

The fire starts when two logs meet.

They barely touch.

Close enough to draw juice from the embers,
enough apart so every tongue moves
freely.

       In a little while time changes the relation.
       One loses in the fire more than the other.

I'll step back.

       You
move an inch forward.

Meditation

Traveling back forty-five light years
through the middle of
your forehead;

tumbling over the edge of the medieval
ocean until you are
merely a

point of light in a black universe,
an absolute elsewhere,
an ovum,

a picture of an ovum on a black page
magnified a billion
times;

feathering off from cushions of sun,
you wake up laughing,
your laugh

tickles the edge of the galaxy,
waiting to be born,
to be

Lament for a Yiddish Poet

Jacob Glatstein, 1896-1971

1.

I want to fasten you inside my head.
Where else can you go now?

I'm sending you my strength,
I said on the telephone.

The telephone wires were laughing at us.

Words are all you left me:
they stroke my cheek, thrust under my hand

like kittens. I heard you shouting, you were angry.
But now I know you were frightened

and didn't want to die
here, at the edge of the desert,

where you struck voices out of rock.

2.

They put you in a pine box
under a star of David
and a few red roses.

The room was breathless
as a grave,
busy with worms.

You stood at the door watching
the coffinbirds peck at the poet.
And quickly left.

3.

In the air, on the wide sky,
you write from right to left,
dark and sunny,
sending me messages.

                    Adam and Eve
are lazing in a pool of blue,
waiting to begin.

Where are you?

                    With a Word,
with a flock of words dense as starlings
you wheel across the sun,
naming the first creatures
in a cantata of light earth sea.

4.

You kissed the face of despair.

I may live to be a hundred, you said,
but I will be dead for centuries.

The faces of all the children, the dead,
the burned, the living, the murdered,
the unborn, are lifted up,
are waiting for your kiss.
For the mother-tongue of rain.

Castoff Skin

She lay in her girlish sleep at ninety-six,
small as a twig.
Pretty good figure

for an old lady, she said to me once.
Then she crawled away, leaving
a tiny stretched transparence

behind her. When I kissed her paper cheek
I thought of the snake,
of his quick motion.

Passover 1970

1.

Athens and Jerusalem   cities of my being   the faces
on your streets are my face   the houses   the rooms inside
the houses   the beds inside the rooms are places   where I
was born   made love   took in your seed

2.

A child of many wars,
how is it my tongue
speaks only the vocabulary of peace?

3.

Now it is time to move out of the narrow space.
The I is the starting place, never the arrival.
The journey outward begins now

4.

Inside Agamemnon's beehive tomb,
the stones,
square and heavy,
fit cleverly together.

The king was laid inside,
a bled shell
once warm to the hands
of his wife.

He was practical,

he traded
his child's life
for fair winds, for war.

Thieves have emptied his tomb.
He did great harm.
And was harmed.
Words   Stones   A cool air

5.

When I was pregnant in the Athens prison, the colonels
beat the soles of my feet with sticks. I asked them
to be careful of the baby. They laughed and said
Another one like you? Soft and arrogant? And beat me more.
Afterwards I lay, unable to walk, weeping in my cell. In
        the dark
I felt a sudden gush between my thighs, and knew
        that I had lost my child

6.

Tigers roam the streets. A crow
snuffs out the sun.
                        Babies
tilt with hairpins at the president,
who scoops them up and stuffs them
in his smile

7.

Pharaoh's horses were closing in behind us.
We shouted and dodged in the dark, stumbling down
        to the beach,
shoving aside even our fathers and children,

trampled, half-drowning, cursing our foolish escape
        from Egypt
when Moses said:
        Stand still, my people. I must think what to do.
        Stand still. I will not let you perish.
        O Lord, you created the earth
        and the water that covers the earth—
        how can I, a mere man,
        separate the sea,
        reverse your plan,
        and give my people a safe path
        to the other side?
        Help me.

8.

Leaving for war, the husband ties his shoes
tightly, confirming the miles between
her bed, his chair.

                    Masada falls.

Lilacs fill the air.
Surviving lovers, barefoot,
multiply.

from THE MARRIAGE WIG
(1968)

A Spider on My Poem

Black one,
I was going to frighten you away,
but now I beg you,
stay!
You're what I need.
This poem needs real legs, faster than the eye.
And a belly with magic string in it
made from spit,
designed to catch and hold whatever flies by.
Also, the uninvited way
you came, boldly, fast as a spider,
till you paused all real in the middle of the page.
Everything I need.
Please stay.

Tall Grasses

Now too I hold my arms up
when grasses grow higher than waist-high
and the shadow still runs out of me
      crying, a child of six, lost in the grasses,
      and I taste the tears of green saliva
from a bent blade scratching my thigh

The green is too high. Like the hostile fingers
the day I saw my mother cry
in the mirror, saw her lost in her weather,
      lost in a field of hurricane,
      lost in a jungle of blades like knives
where the grasses grow too high

Spring

When I was
thirteen I
believed that
the mailman
had sperm on
his hands and
if he touched
me I would
be pregnant
if he brushed
against me
in the hall
from my pores would sprout twigs branches leaves
buds blossoms unfurling I'd be an apple
tree in my white wedding dress swelling
the room until flowers exploded into the street
and rose up filling the sky blowsy with
fruit to come

Listening to grownups quarreling,

standing in the hall against the
wall with my little brother, blown
like leaves against the wall by their
voices, my head like a pingpong ball
between the paddles of their anger:
I knew what it meant
to tremble like a leaf.

Cold with their wrath, I heard
the claws of the rain
pounce. Floods
poured through the city,
skies clapped over me,
and I was shaken, shaken
like a mouse
between their jaws.

Persephone Travels Back to Hell, as Arranged

So long as this old subway keeps going,
I'm all right,
but it's the sudden stopping, the pause
in the middle of no air, nowhere
that gasps me.

Traveling back to a first rape,
cold and self-kidnapped,
I feel blunt and dulled.
It seemed truer, the first violence.

                    *

Snatched up in my father's Packard, his ancient troika,
crouched by his side,
we went plunging through the curving
Vermont hills
at what I thought was a fast clip, forty
miles an hour;
learning winter, forced to surrender
to one direction,
I learned the high glee of being driven,
ridden by a man.

The road ate itself up like a snake with its tail
in its mouth,
the world was one great perilous snake of a
roller coaster.

                    *

Now in my smart new winter coat,
orange, the color of sunsets,
and a hat made from a lamb

slaughtered half a world away;
packed lightly in one suitcase
so I won't need a porter,
I buy passage on his bankrupt line.

My gratitude to the black guts of the earth,
my thanks to this submachine taking me into the tunnel.
I brush kisses from my fingertips to all bats, roots, moles,
all blind and upsidedown things
squatting and squinting in the waiting dark.

Rachel Waking

She's in a well,
the walls covered with
slippery moss between
wet stones.
Under the water asleep,
holding her breath.
The clock strikes,
shooting her to the surface.

Her nose and the top of her head break through to air.
She scatters the scum lazing on the surface, the dragon-
fly resting, the flat leaf of autumn.

She climbs,
sliding up the slippery walls,
dreams clinging to her ankles.
She wants to fall back.

But up there standing in crisp grass, Jacob
waits by the well, leaning his elbow against
the day, tossing idly in his hands
her brand new morning.

Cutting the Jewish Bride's Hair

It's to possess more than the skin
that those old world Jews
exacted the hair of their brides.
> Good husband, lover of the Torah,
> does the calligraphy of your bride's hair
> interrupt your page?

Before the clownish friction of flesh
creating out of nothing
a mockup of its begetters,
a miraculous puppet of God,
you must first divorce her from her vanity.

She will snip off her pride,
cut back her appetite to be devoured,
she will keep herself well braided,
her love's furniture will not endanger you,
> but this little amputation
> will shift the balance of the universe.

The Marriage Wig

*If you're going to marry, make sure you
first know whom you're going to divorce.*
—YIDDISH PROVERB

1.

The Mishnah says I blind you with my hair,
that when I bind it in a net
my fingers waylay my friends;
that in a close house I shake loose
the Pleiades into your kitchen.

How can I let you see me, past and future,
blemishes and dust? Must I
shear away my hair and wear
the wig the wisemen say? Will you
receive me, rejoice me, take me for your wall?

2.

Once upon a time I wrote a boy
into my calendar of weddings. We lived
in a gargoyle house with many eyes.
Snow furred the street lamps. Inside
we had our wine, one pot, an innocent fire.

Now the gargoyle house is gone. On a tree
is the orphan number, forty-nine, meaning
49, a house, a marriage, a time
scythed clean, crunched to powder, flat
as a grave, as though we'd never been.

Let me apologize for that lost number.

3.

Let me apologize for all the faces
I've worn, none of them my own.
See me in my glass. A ghost looks back,
a witty ghost, who counterfeits my mask,
wearing a marriage wig made of my hair.

Inside, I'm threaded on a passion
taut as a tightrope. Strip away the hair,
the tooth, the wrinkle, the obscene
cartoon that decades scrawl—
underneath I'm naked as a nun.

Ripeness

You wake up feeling
like an oven
where bread
has just been baked.

All night the yeast rose
and at dawn
you baked the bread,
a round full loaf.

Reunion

*After the division the two parts of man, each
desiring the other half, came together, and threw
their arms about one another eager to grow into one . . .*
—Plato, SYMPOSIUM, translated by B. Jowett

when your skin is strapped
to my bones, when I breathe
with your breath, wear your small
of the back, smile, eyelashes,
I'll be home again:

but I might cry for your marrow,
parching for your tongue,
and you might still turn away,
fearing the smart of my going,
so slowly grows our grafting—

until your sex takes mine,
finally, as it was
before the beginning, before
the pregods envied us
and split in two our one

David's Breath

let's celebrate the
breath and airs
of love. David's
mouth, pastures of
honeysuckle, the nape
of his baby
neck, crops of
clover. Leda's hair
newly washed, a
thicket of balsam.
Under your arm
a decanter of
spices, the slope
of your torso,
newly cut wood.
And your sex
spilled over, like
barnfresh milk, like
warm brandy, like
David's breath

Summer Thunderstorms

She walked bravely down the country road
every late afternoon

but she was frightened before it began.
Mountain shadows had moved

around her all day, a young bride
whose mother had now grown old.

Womb shapes gathered over the mountains, tongues of
electric snakes licked

the sky, just as she came back to the house,
lit the fragile lamp,

and began to get the meal. The house had stood
two hundred years, but brides

can't believe they'll live in history.
When the roof seemed to split

with the first crack of the daily storm, her throat
became cement. The table

was only half set, the potatoes just
boiling, but she sank
sank again into the sky's cauldron.

Sitting for a Picture

The painter
narrows his
eye, measures
along his
finger, looks
at her up-
sidedown then
backwards in
a mirror.

Not touched the
girl on the
couch begins
to wear his
grammar. Per-
spective flat-
tens her curves
buttock brow
she becomes
more than her
self, catch for
a palette.

She gives off
faint power
like perfume
or buddha
she sits in
his eye like
an apple.

The Act of Bread

*Some practice is required to knead quickly, but
the motion once acquired will never be forgotten.*
—"Water Bread," THE BOSTON COOKING-SCHOOL
COOK BOOK by Fannie Merritt Farmer, 1898

That happy multiplying
should have lasted all night.
But long before dawn
my batter crawled up the walls.
The trouble was, I let my secret
passion run into my thumbs:
into my own
flour yeast water I plunged my lust
up to the elbows—pounding the white
buttocks of my children, turning
their rosy heels; kneading the
side, loin, groin of him
to whom I long owed this caressing.

But before I could give form to desire,
invented flesh outran me.
It towered in my biggest bowl,
flowed over table shelves floor
till I scooped it up, frightened at my power,
and tried to hide it in a paper
bag. In an hour
it burst the side, climbed
out the window, through the door.

If I had baked that dough,
a crumb would serve as aphrodisiac:
one slice of bread
would people a continent.

      But in panic
I carried it outside, bucket by bucket,
and gave it to the cold November morning.

She Doesn't Want to Bring the Tides in Any More

Every time she tugs the sun across the sky
some old wound
comes apart at the seams.
But housekeeping by the clock means keeping
every star prompt. She puffs along,
blowing a strand of graying hair out of her eyes,
but she gets each planet to its place
on time. She bruises a hip
moving all this furniture around.

She steers clouds, fans winds, and slices
or mends the moon, according to the day.
Worst of all is bringing in the tides.
One hand brings them in on one side,
the other pushes them away;
                           while her knee
keeps the tipped earth spinning on its axis
precariously.

No wonder she went away and sat down on a sand dune,
wishing she were grass.
If she sits still long enough,
rain will come to her.

All My Bicycles Are Emily Dickinson

Perfectly oiled, her tires tight with twenty pounds of air,
delighting in her moving parts, she mows
a narrow ribbon up the gravel. In low,
aware of every separate pebble, we make smaller
revolutions, fighting gravity all the way.

Out on the flat, we shift to second, raising our eyes
and seeing the bird's-eye map of leaves, striated bark
under the blue proscenium. Our spokes
make a girlish click click as we lope down
the wide highway, watching everything.

Now in high, we start to take off. Leaning my soles
on her pedals, I lift slightly off her seat,
letting the wind take us. I name her
Emily. And now she remembers how once
God pumped his floods of warm diamonds into her.

Sister Pharaoh

Hatshepsut, old girl, old friend,
man-woman, bearded Pharaoh,
we women too pasted on beards
and said we were kings.
We brought lullaby rules of commerce to the state,
we raised temples and wrote hieroglyphs
and got the men
to erect an obelisk for us.

Hatshepsut,
you crouch in the silent hall of tombs,
trying to be a riddle.
But we can see through your beard.
Beneath your terrible crown of upper and lower Egypt,
beneath your archaic stone smile,
our milk has turned to powder,
our breasts are two inches of dust.

The Nun Cuts Her Hair

The nun
bald as
a uniform
offers her
hair to
her endless
Bridegroom.

And He
caressing as
air as
the sea
remembers winter
remembers
her hair.

Dancing at Delphi

Ribboning down the unpaved highway
from Delphi to Arachova,
a skein of men and women
full of cheese, wine,
Saturday night love,

lifts you off the ground.
Through their bodies,
into their fingers,
the earth leaps upward
into you.

Noonday in the Plaka

Walking up from a bulletpocked house—
the smell of urine, dust
rises from the crackedlazy
sidewalk, fresh
bread from some
kitchen and crisp
entrails frying.

Up the sheet metal street,
each jagged house is
pinged by white light.
The organ grinder plays *o sole mio*
on his gingerbread organ, then
the death dance
from Zalonghou.

Public Images

THAT WOMAN HOLDING OUT HER HAND
is lying under
rafters, sand, stone,
bricks, sticks
of wood, a giant
girder, a mountain.
Only her head and one hand
are free.
Her face holds
continents
of pleading.

THE BOYISH POLITICIAN
naive and human, his
tie askew,
seems to be explaining.
His jacket is torn,
his collar all in motion.
They have poured cement
into one shoe
making his foot
immobile.

AN APOLOGY TO THE LIBERATED INMATES:
my clean underwear
makes it difficult for me
to understand you.
At what point did you
stop filing your nails,
stop planning what to have for dinner?

Peeled from my house, my skin,

would I be
raw like you
sick like you
an angry
harp of bones?

OUR NEXT DOOR SURVIVOR
lives above the waist
strapped on a bed
among lilacs, tulips,
suburban cherry blossoms.
Her legs belong to those
black woods where
Jewish children
march, trying not to
cry at the guards,
at the sourfaced trees.

THE LATE ASTRONAUT IN THE BOSTON GLOBE
grins foolishly at the unmanned
camera. Behind him
the earthglobe dangles.
His shoulderblade
blots out the map of Africa,
his earlobe overcomes
the China sea.
We've caught him,
tipsy in space,
walking nowhere.

Let's give him
burial toys—
two planets,
one for each hand,

let's paint
an Egyptian eye
to steer his ship
as he passes
our old sky.

Her Delirium

The old lady
(a child of seven)
cried in her sleep
Stop beating me!
Zu hilfe!
Zu hilfe!
In the dark cellar
her sons had murdered . . .
And the policeman was punishing . . .

The bright light
slid down the white bed
and the little girl
saw her wrinkled arm,
her withered knee.
Which is me, she cried,
which body is mine,
and why are they beating
an old lady of eighty-nine?

The Mark

Grandpa, when you
lay dying, your throat
wrapped in bandages,
I came to see you
after school.

You wrote kindly
on a scrap of paper,
What's new? and I,
blindly, Today
I got an A.

You smiled at me
for that schoolgirl boast.
You already knew
what I couldn't see.

And I'm ashamed,
still ashamed.

Dead Center

for John Holmes

        A thin fox
sidled by with his stingy shadow.
Bees hung in air,
each like a chandelier,
hot pine pinched my nostrils.

You sat up in bed
wrestling with the fox's silence,
it isn't time, it isn't time.
I looked at your face with the sharp regret
a mother feels for her child
sleeping after the day's war.

They broke flowers on your coffin,
knowing you weren't there. The sun came out
and all your faces flared for a moment:
you weren't there.
I'll beat my poem into a trap
for the stingy fox, to prove
that you were here.

In the Smoking Car

That hatless chewed woman sending me messages
with her eyes, what does she know about me?
That I've had my last child, that my
clocks are stopping? That love still comes to me
like birthdays or Christmas, and a brushed kiss
can be a whole concert?

She is grayer than I, more toothless,
but she grins like a sister.
Do my sins show?
                What deception
does she see through me?
I shrink from her wrinkles, her sporty air,
her certain knowledge, older than cats,
that I am pretending, pretending, pretending.

Old Houses

I wear this house like a barrel
to cover my struts
and I see:
>the plaster's getting veined.
>Tender clapboards won't stand
>too much more rain.
>Inside
>the wallpaper's crepey
>where the storm came in.

Looking out from inside
it's hard to tell:
will a coat of spanking paint
make the trim seem new again?

I've seen other women preen
to the image in their eyes,
picturing moviestar lips,
a dashing lilt to the head,
>while in the mirror
>looking back
>an old mask
>props up its wrinkles
>with a kissed out mouth.

But I feel like a virgin in the dark.
I hear my voice like a child's
enter the telephone
and come out no older.

>How come this new me
>is looking out of an old house?

I Become My Grandfather

Grandpa, I
want to tell you
simply:
that picture of you,
the handsome one with
curly gray hair,
amorous eyes,
arms folded in satisfaction—

I have looked
at you since I was
a little girl:
my grandfather.

Today I thought:
he's like some friend of mine,
a man I could love,
a sweetheart.
And reckoned
I'm now older
than your picture
by one year.

Departures

The buses stand in slips like ocean liners.
I scan the driver's face for signs of kindness.

    Rachel, now taller than I, once asked
    (before she had breasts, when she thought she was
        Snow White):

    How does a man look to a dragon?

    And answered:
    the man is very small,
    the dragon doesn't care about him at all.
    He'd crush him with his toenail.

Brave as an eggshell,
I've come to see her off.

A bulky girl stands by
with stonehenge ankles.
Sorrow seems to fill her like cement.

Rachel squeezes into the monster Greyhound,
clutching her suitcase.
I stand in the shadows.

Beside me a tiny Puerto Rican couple
are waiting with their children.
The boy and girl are chalk-faced, hollow-eyed.
They never cry.
The mother looks sixteen, too young to worry.
She holds the little boy slung on her hip,
while under him a spread of urine slowly

stains her skirt.

> Last night, love, when our bodies meshed most
> deeply,
> I touched your face and knew,
> across a highway of nightmare,
> your sudden absence.
> Traveler, you slipped away
> as we lay side by side.
> Come back.

The driver slams his door and starts the motor.

Stonehenge stands alone like stone, crying.

Wrong bus for the Puerto Ricans.

> As the Greyhound backs away
> I blow it an anonymous kiss
> and think I see,
> through the moving dark,
> an answering hand.

You Outlive All Your Diseases Except One

1.

Give me anything of value, the nurse said,
watches, rings, teeth, whatever
is removable, also your eye, leg, hair
no I said and there are no
hairpins on me either, nothing,
nothing, I am stripped
down to my self,
plucked like a chicken, punctured for oblivion,
in anonymous white worn backwards,
wheeled like secondhand goods to a stall.

Strapped under arc lights I see
a dark doctor who says he writes poetry
in Arabic. I sympathize with a kind
anaesthetist who can't find my veins. I halloo
my own doctor who like santa claus
with a black goody for me sends me
raw, split,
sailing into cushions of mercy.

2.

Name me the parts
of cars, pistons, spark plugs, axles,
tires, doors, roof, radiator, categories
of fallibility that will be eaten
by collision, rust, attrition, age
and lie
abandoned by a used car dealer
in a hospital of wrecks.

Grass pushes through that speedy engine.
A lazy beetle
on the steering wheel
turns imperceptibly with the earth's
turning. They have lost their counterpoint of motion.
Gaping like lepers
the old cars freeze
in insufficiency: sky, weeds.

Shoring Up

1.

On a clockless summer afternoon
in a cradle of seahaze
cupped in the palm of a dune
a man sleeps, defenseless as all sleeping creatures are.

Medallion.

I wear that graceful icon
pinned inside my forehead
to ward me against certain disaster.

2.

Last night's explosion blew
the starfish high.
I looked out and saw
sharks swimming in the sky;
the shaken sky
shook my bed.

I pulled in my knees,
saw a hill in Greece
where two small boys
fished in the air for birds.

They cast their lines in the thick gold air
and reeled back finches and starlings.
The cameo sea grinned
as though posing for eternity.

3.

Propelled by old guilts,
cast up on a rocky shore,
I lean propped on my images.

The man sleeps, his buttocks curved like a child
carved on an ivory gem, his fingers
opened out, his tender arc
suspended in my eye.

from BLOOD AND MILK POEMS

(1963)

Stealing Forsythia

I came back with the sun smeared on my hands,
A yellow guilt
Pulled from my neighbor's bush,
Ten yellow branches
Moist with guilt and joy,
Caged in a green vase on the piano top.

Each time I pass my green and stolen prize
I feel again the greening of my years.

I would steal light from any bush,
Rob any blaze from heaven for my vase,
Just as I danced once on your wooden floor,
Naked and sudden,
Whirling you in a waltz,
Or did you whirl me,
Shaking the yellow spring
From rafters winter-stained with penitence?

That's the way I'd always have my guilt,
Sudden, high, a theft of fire, a dance,
A secret flowering of forsythia.

Elevator

This sudden box has boxed me in my life.

Airless, I watch the leapfrog numbers play.
It's a sly trick. They want to make me think
I'm moving to perfection, but

They're wrong. I'm merely standing still.
The floors themselves are moving up and down
While I stand loyal to my gravity.

Down and up the steel girders slide.
All those bricks and not one out of place.
They do this out of ignorance or pride.

I'm standing still. You see it by my face.

Round

I keep my clocks a little fast
so time won't take me by surprise.

Lest crows tread harshly round my eyes
I keep my clocks a little fast.

I push ahead the hands of past
before the future tints my hair.

I race the hours through the air
so time won't take me by surprise.

Before the spider bygone dries
I cobble cobwebs on my last.

I keep my clocks a little fast
so time won't take me by surprise.

Nuns on the Beach

Strewn on the sand, a pride of nuns—
Apart from the herd, adrift on the beach,
Undone to their chins, with legs laid bare—
Spread out their wintry souls to bleach,
Smiled the sun their orisons,
And hid their bandaged hair.

What is the sea to a convent cell?
Sparkle and gulls and toes in sand.
The pride of nuns had a swimming race—
The buoy's gong was a warning bell—
And each with her wimple round her face
Played leapmermaid hand in hand.

And I felt out of place.

The Witch of the Wave

a prescription for a figurehead

That's how my carver made me:
Breasts thrust against the hammer of the sea.

Against is my element:
Driven against salt spray, wind, the jaw of the whale,

Against ice, spindrift, I plow my body's death.

Wrenched from mortal wood
I suffered the pain of birth.

With each chip
That fell on the sawdust floor my forest fell from me.

To this the birth and loss of any voyage is nothing.

The head must be carved in such a way it will
not hold water.

The body, curved in eagerness for flight, must fit
snugly to the cutwater, fit the curve of the bow.

So did he bend my tree.

Now I spring at the tide, haul crews of whalers,
Anvil against the wave.

When I plunge in the storm, I rise like a diver, sheering
All water from me.

My hair steams with foam, my paint gnawed
By the maw of salt.

Tethered to the world's weight, I raise the hull,
My face high to the gale.

Gulls know me. Dolphins
Dabble in my wake.

Splintered and beached,
Shipwreck is not my end. I bequeath my lucky bones

To some young sailor
Bound for his next horizon.

Touching a fragment of me in his pocket,
He touches pain, danger, phosphorescent joy, knowing

I bribe the ocean for his safe return.

Song for a Vigil

The bells all suddenly are nine
Be light my leaf the dark is bold

Love hung all night on a sagging vine
His grape a burr, his leaf a spine,
But now the clocks are ringing nine

Love shook all night in heavy cold,
His song a cry, his kisses old,
Be light my leaf the dark is bold

He comes with feet as bare as mine
And helps me stamp the bitter wine,
For all the clocks are ringing nine.

Be light my leaf the dark is bold.

The Old Man's Mistress

The two old heads
on each side of his young deathbed, mistress and wife,
met headon. He asked for the Bible.
Perhaps it was to prove he was right, after all.
But his curly hair proved it, and the women
who loved him, and his graygreen eyes, and now he was dying,
by choice. The thing he insisted on,
choice.

Cancer, pogroms, ignorance, gangrene
he chose the thing he was to die of.
It could have been too much love.
He chose a broadhipped blondhaired mistress
with Scandinavia in her eyes, far from
the racket of his four sons in the tenement,
far from the immigrant wife who scrubbed his stairs,
far from the Russian soldiers who took his oldest
brother to Moscow to be a goy.

She heard
the lullaby in his voice. She had slapped
her old husband, twenty years before,
for his feudal lechery, and left.
That was her choice.

And then she chose him, Jacob.
He let nothing come of her womb.
She wept when she saw
me, his granddaughter, and her would-be
greatgrandchildren.
But she baked bread
and scrubbed his sweet body in a bathtub

set in the Connecticut grass,
and learned a few Yiddish words,
and outlived him.

       I am my grandmother
with her four sons, her outliving patience,
her patient hate.

       I am my grandfather,
loved beyond usual lot,
stealing his delight.

       I am my grandfather's mistress,
tending the alien land he left,
with no face for the face she loves,
                dying
alone with her lovely bones, her only choice.

The Peacock Screams

A hidden peacock in the yard at night
Burns like a moonlit fish, an emperor crowned,
And waits to flash his gold embroidered tail,
And waits to spread the palette of his eye,
And prick my dark with iridescent fire.

But dark was once when bright Ionian boys
Dove for pearls in midnight water. Now
They dive for shipwreck.
                              Salt has closed their eyes,

So bury all my peacocks deep at sea,
Their color is the shape of sailors drowned.

Aubade

When sleep kaleidoscopes and every tree
Rings out before a cannonball of sun
Sharp music shatters for the birds to sing,
Breaking their bits of glass upon the street,
Green glass, mean clatter, lovers' mourning bells.

Your kiss invented me, but I forget,
So constellate my sky with stars again:
Planets burn brief beside our tides of blood.

The Lost Steps

What the son wishes to forget, the grandson wishes to remember.
MARCUS LEE HANSON

Snow fell when my young grandfather arrived,
Behind him Moscow, Eden, Athens, Rome,
Bareheaded, eighteen, and a wandering Jew.

Snow covered up his footsteps leading home.

Defiant of history, he laughed his way
Through passover streets, under each arm a loaf
Of leavened bread. A forgetting snow that day.

   *

The first snow was the laying on of hands,
Blessing and naming, while Eve looked up to see
The white erasure hide her Adam's land.

How she had come, how gone, when Jahweh smiled
Blew drifting in her brain. She turned again
Back to her dishes and her hungry child.

And those old men rocking round their ark,
Beautiful in their beards, prayed all that fell,
Manna or snow, be Jahweh's favoring mark.

And Leda knew, when feathers fell like snow,
The thunderous wings of God in bright sunrise,
And threw her arms around his swansdown neck

And served him in his passionate disguise.
But in God's ravishing, Mary had wrung
Her hands beneath the bird who brought the sky

To cover her lament. Not knowing why,
Except she thought she saw her baby hung,
Shrunken, from the rafters of the world.

*

Was that my garden where I sang innocence?
Was that my cross that nailed the patient Jew?
Were those my thunderous wings? Was that my swan?

I cannot bend my knee.
All, all is gone.
I live on the charity of history.

Part ark, part swan, part cross over her hair,
My daughter stands before a holy fount.
Snow falls before my eyes. I cannot see.

I cannot bend my knee. I would not dare.

Her Life Was in My Hands

From Sappho to the girl upon the moon
Sitting three centuries from now, I burn
With hot winds from the
Gutters of the earth.

We three were swimmers poised to dive
In catastrophic seas
Where down beneath the surface of those eyes,
Where worlds pull, where dead stars yearn,
My wrecked and whitened timber
Lies embraced in fern.

And she who from the cold sphere gazes down
Weeps to see me swim through outer space,
My very veins translated
To pregnant universe.

And she who gazes up through tidal trees,
Against the ocean's palm that weighs me down,
Cries me to rise, still dreaming to remember
The flooding terror of the moon's embrace,
The birth to come, the sting
Of comets on my face.

The Flowering Skull

Monger of melting snow, the lovegod death
Cried up my avenue, fresh melting snow,
Who'll buy my melting snow?

Young hair will fall, ripe pear will crawl with beetle,
Doors rot and latches rust, tall lilies fall,
All tearless, windless fall.

My jagged heart, pinned at the root upon
The very bone, my season's jagged heart
Hoards death and distance. Heart

To hawker of the snow: I'll trade you death
And distance for the promise under snow,
The infant season stirring under snow,
One season's rose for all your melting snow,
I'll trade you, trade you snow for melting snow.

Antiphonal

that first pang of air
daggered me fish to man.

                Child of my dark, you
                And I were almost one.

all the walls fell away.
nothing held me

                Now my body and I are
                Almost two, part

but the giant light,
and I fell, or flew

                Catapult for your despair,
                And, for your anger and alarm,

then drew my brandnew breath

                Part suckling heart.

and screamed.

The Sea Flower

To the changeling coral and pearl
The moon is a huge purple plum.
But the shadow under the kelp,
When his time has ripened to come,
Prays through the wave's fierce furl
And the seaweed's solemn ballet
For the moon's sweet harvest help
And the bitter power to pray.

The Phoenix

A flaming phoenix came to rest
Beside my tiny nursling's nest,
Womb-warm,
Womb-blessed,

He snapped his wings of fire and cried
The world is full of claws outside,
And tall,
And wide,

The sky is turning golden red
And I have come with flames outspread
And Hallelujah in my head
To toss you from your easy bed,
To toss you from your bed.

My Daughter the Cypress

Sleep, little daughter, I'll plant you a tree
Even as grandmother planted for me,
One tiny sapling more for the hill
Where two little cousins are flourishing still.

Sleep, sleep, dream of the sea,
Your cradle's a caïque, your tree, your tree
Will be a mast to take you from me
Grown for the boy who fells you free.

Sleep, sleep, the tree is yet small,
An infant tree, not three years tall,
It mocks its sisters, flutters its boughs,
Hush, hush, it rains, it snows,

Summer suns lengthen your hair,
You grow tall, you move with care,
And from the sea bright blue and white,
A sailor whistles in the night.

But sleep, sleep, not yet, not yet—
The hull is carved, the mast is set—
Sleep one more night in Arcady,
My little girl, my cypress tree.

Touro Synagogue

As to an unknown lover I returned
To my father's land, a shifting land, now jeweled
And satined like a bride, a holy ark.

A stranger to his house, I heard my talk
More friendly to the twelve Ionic trees
Than to the tribes of Israel, more shy

To celebrate this birthday than to die.
White and perfect, starred with candlelight,
The sacred chamber held a secret stair.

The heart's escape leads out to everywhere,
Nowhere, but dreams still find a certain black
Connecticut hill.   My grandfather stands tall

And wraps me in his cemetery cloak,
Encircles me against the nightmare chill,
Till gowned in fear I follow with his ghost

Through village, town, down through the midnight past
To a second son reading by candlelight
Forbidden books that set his future free,

To an immigrant tender in his blasphemy,
Bold, repentant, joyful against death,
Rich in gesture, eloquent as earth.

Ignorant of all, I catch my breath
To hear the sharp crack of the shattered cup.
Driven to live, I grope to gather up

The windless torch of love, my tribe's rebirth.